DECLARE YOUR DAY

365 Prophetic Declarations for Breakthrough and Victory

ROMA WATERMAN

©Roma Waterman 2024

All materials contained in this book are the copyrighted property of Roma Waterman trading as I Was Carried Pty Ltd. To reproduce, republish, post, modify, distribute or display material from this publication, you must first obtain permission for the author at:

Roma Waterman
P O Box 288
Warrandyte, Victoria
Melbourne, Australia 3113
roma@romawaterman.com
www.romawaterman.com
www.training.romawaterman.com

Cover Artwork by: Joshua Halls, Roar Kingdom Creative

All Scripture quotations, unless otherwise indicated, are taken from the Holy Bible, New International Version®, NIV®. Copyright ©1973, 1978, 1984, 2011 by Biblica, Inc.TM Used by permission of Zondervan, and New King James Version®. Copyright © 1982 by Thomas Nelson. Used by permission. All rights reserved.

All rights reserved worldwide. www.zondervan.comThe "NIV" and "New International Version" are trademarks registered in the United States Patent and Trademark Office by Biblica, Inc.TM

Published by: I Was Carried Pty Ltd
Distributed by: I Was Carried Pty Ltd

INTRODUCTION

Have you ever noticed how a single word can change everything? A doctor speaks "cancer-free," and joy floods the room. A child says "Mama" for the first time, and a parent's heart melts. A simple "yes" at the altar transforms two lives forever. Words have power—they create, they heal, they transform, and they can even set the course of our lives.

I remember the morning everything changed for me. Overwhelmed with life's challenges during the covid lockdowns, I found myself mindlessly scrolling through social media feeling so moved by the hopelessness many across the world were feeling. There was so much fear even from believers. I felt frustrated, not sure how to help, and honestly not sure how I was feeling myself about what was happening! That's when I heard the gentle whisper of the Holy Spirit: "What are you declaring? It's time to speak life!"

This simple question stopped me in my tracks. I realized my compassion for the world had been consumed by fear, exhaustion, and limitations that were not just around me but all around the world. That day marked the beginning of a promise to the Lord to use social media in a way that spoke His hope and life into every situation.

I learned first hand the power of biblical declarations, as I began to post every day a prophetic declaration of hope. I would sit with the Lord the night before and ask Him what was on his heart to post the next morning. Upon request from many on social media, that journey turned into a book called *Declare – Declarations of Hope For The Modern Soul*. It was a completely unexpected journey that would not only change my life but has also led to the creation of this book. I received so many testimonies during that time of people being transformed by the declarations that pulled them out of hopelessness and fear and I want to keep it going! I began to ask myself, "What would it look like to prophesy using scripture every day of the year?" And that's what you are holding in your hands right now.

Why Declarations Matter

When God created the universe, He didn't think it into existence—He spoke it into being. "And God said, 'Let there be light,' and there was light" (Genesis 1:3). Made in His image, we too carry the power of creative speech. The Bible tells us that we have what we say (Mark 11:23), that our words can bring death or life (Proverbs 18:21), and that we overcome by the word of our testimony (Revelation 12:11).

Think about it: many major moves of God in Scripture involved declaration. Moses declared freedom to the Israelites. Joshua declared victory at Jericho. David declared triumph over Goliath before the stone ever left his sling. Mary declared, "Be it unto me according to your word," and the course of human history was forever changed.

More Than Positive Thinking

This book isn't about positive thinking or wishful speaking. It's about aligning our words with God's Word—partnering with

Heaven's perspective to see Heaven's possibilities manifest in our lives. These declarations aren't magic formulas; they are tools of transformation that help us renew our minds and align our hearts with God's truth.

Each daily declaration in this book has been carefully crafted to:

- Root you deeply in Scripture
- Align your words with God's promises
- Build your faith through consistent proclamation
- Create an atmosphere for miracles in your daily life
- Transform your thinking to match Heaven's perspective

How to Use This Book

Each day, you'll find a powerful declaration followed by a corresponding Scripture. I encourage you to:

1. Read the declaration aloud each morning
2. Meditate on the accompanying Scripture
3. Personalize the declaration for your specific situation
4. Journal about any insights or breakthroughs if you have time
5. Repeat the declaration throughout your day

And friends, let me prepare you - some days, the declarations will feel natural and powerful. Other days, they may feel like you're speaking to mountains that haven't yet moved. That's okay. Keep declaring. Keep believing. Keep speaking life!

A Year of Transformation

As you embark on this 365-day journey, know that you're not just reading a book—you are participating in a divine partnership with Holy Spirit. Every declaration is an opportunity to align your words with God's Word, your thoughts with God's thoughts, and your expectations with God's promises.

The prophet Isaiah shared this promise, "So shall my word be that goes out from my mouth; it shall not return to me empty, but it shall accomplish that which I purpose, and shall succeed in the thing for which I sent it" (Isaiah 55:11). God's Word never returns void, and when we declare His truth over our lives, we position ourselves for supernatural breakthrough.

Are you ready to begin? Turn the page and start your journey of prophetic declaration. Your words have power, and your future is waiting to be spoken into existence.

Let's prophesy together!

With faith and expectation,

Roma Waterman

CHAPTER 1

THE POWER OF DECLARATIONS: SPEAKING LIFE INTO YOUR FUTURE

There is profound power in the words we speak. Just as God spoke the universe into existence, declaring "Let there be light" (Genesis 1:3), our words have the ability to shape our reality and transform our lives. When we align our declarations with God's Word, we partner with His creative power to bring Heaven's possibilities into our earthly experience.

The Biblical Foundation

The Scripture tells us, "Death and life are in the power of the tongue, and those who love it will eat its fruits" (Proverbs 18:21). This isn't merely poetic language—it's a spiritual principle that echoes throughout the Bible. When Joshua led the Israelites around Jericho, it wasn't their military might that brought down the walls; it was their obedience and a shout of faith from their lips (Joshua 6:20).

Consider the story of the Roman centurion who came to Jesus. His understanding of authority led him to declare, "Just say the word, and my servant will be healed" (Matthew 8:8). Jesus marveled at his faith, demonstrating the power of believing and declaring God's authority over our circumstances.

Modern-Day Testament

Smith Wigglesworth, often called the "Apostle of Faith," was known to read nothing but the Bible for the last 40 years of his life. He famously said, "I am not moved by what I see. I am not moved by what I feel. I am moved only by what I believe." Each morning, he would read God's Word and declare it over his life and ministry. His impact, decades after his death continues to influence millions today.

Nick Vujicic, born without arms and legs, could have let his circumstances dictate his life's story. Instead, he chose to declare God's truth over his life. His favorite Scripture, "I can do all things through Christ who strengthens me" (Philippians 4:13), became more than just words—it became his living testimony. Today, he inspires millions worldwide, proving that our declarations, backed by faith, can overcome any limitation. Our words change us. Words fuelled with God's power will transform us.

The Science

Modern science has begun to catch up with what Scripture has always taught. Neuroplasticity research shows that our thoughts and words literally reshape our brain pathways. Dr. Caroline Leaf, a cognitive neuroscientist explains how positive declarations aligned with Scripture can actually rewire our neural pathways and transform our thinking patterns. Incredible stuff!

Making Declarations Work for You

The prophet Ezekiel stood in a valley of dry bones and declared life when everything around him spoke of death (Ezekiel 37). Like him, we're called to speak life even when circumstances suggest otherwise. As Paul writes, we are to "call those things which do not exist as though they did" (Romans 4:17).

The Power of Persistence

Consider the persistent widow in Luke 18. Jesus used her story to teach us about never giving up in prayer and declaration. Similarly, Elijah prayed and declared seven times before the rain came (1 Kings 18:43-44). Sometimes, our declarations require persistence before we see manifestation. Don't give up!

A Daily Practice

Charles Spurgeon once said, "A Bible that's falling apart usually belongs to someone who isn't." Make your declarations a daily practice, not just a sporadic exercise. Let them be the first fruits of your morning, setting the tone for your entire day.

Remember the words of Job: "You will decree a thing, and it will be established for you" (Job 22:28). When we declare God's Word over our lives, we're not merely speaking positive thoughts—we're aligning ourselves with the creative power that formed the universe.

Through intentional, Scripture-based declarations, you're not just speaking words into the air; you're partnering with God's creative power to shape your future. As you embark on this 365-day journey of declarations, remember that you're following in the footsteps of countless faithful believers who discovered that when God's Word is in your mouth, transformation is on the horizon!

Be blessed as you declare the life, hope, love and power of Jesus daily in your life!

January 1

Today, I walk in God's peace, knowing He is my refuge and strength.

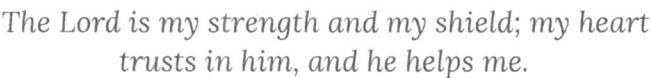

The Lord is my strength and my shield; my heart trusts in him, and he helps me.

(Psalm 28:7)

January 2

I declare divine favor over every step I take today.

For you bless the righteous, O Lord; you cover him with favor as with a shield.

(Psalm 5:12)

January 3

I speak life over my circumstances, knowing God is working all things for my good.

And we know that in all things God works for the good of those who love him.

(Romans 8:28)

January 4

Today, I choose faith over fear, knowing God is with me.

Be strong and courageous. Do not be afraid; do not be discouraged, for the Lord your God will be with you wherever you go.

(Joshua 1:9)

January 5

I declare that my mind is filled with God's thoughts and my heart is aligned with His purpose.

Do not conform to the pattern of this world, but be transformed by the renewing of your mind.

(Romans 12:2)

January 6

I prophesy abundance and provision, knowing the Lord supplies all my needs.

And my God will meet all your needs according to the riches of his glory in Christ Jesus.
(Philippians 4:19)

January 7

I am more than a conqueror through Christ, and I declare victory in every area of my life.

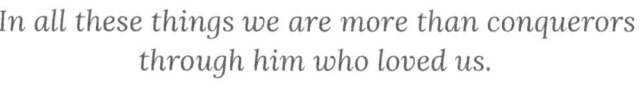

In all these things we are more than conquerors through him who loved us.

(Romans 8:37)

January 8

Today, I choose to rest in God's goodness, trusting His plans for my life.

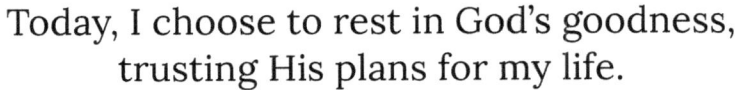

The Lord will fight for you; you need only to be still.
(Exodus 14:14)

January 9

I declare open doors and divine opportunities as I walk in obedience to God's voice.

See, I have placed before you an open door that no one can shut.

(Revelation 3:8)

January 10

My words today will bring life and blessing to those around me.

The tongue has the power of life and death, and those who love it will eat its fruit.

(Proverbs 18:21)

January 11

I declare that God's strength carries me through every challenge I face today.

I can do all this through him who gives me strength.
(Philippians 4:13)

January 12

Today, I declare breakthrough and victory in areas where I've been waiting for answers.

The Lord your God is the one who goes with you to fight for you against your enemies to give you victory.

(Deuteronomy 20:4)

January 13

I speak peace over my mind and heart, trusting that God is in control.

You will keep in perfect peace those whose minds are steadfast, because they trust in you.

(Isaiah 26:3)

January 14

I declare that I am fearfully and wonderfully made, and I walk in my God-given identity.

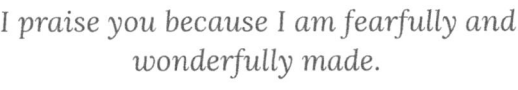

I praise you because I am fearfully and wonderfully made.

(Psalm 139:14)

January 15

I speak healing over my body, mind, and soul, declaring that I am whole in Jesus.

He heals the brokenhearted and binds up their wounds.

(Psalm 147:3)

January 16

I declare that I am walking in alignment with God's purpose for my life.

The steps of a good man are ordered by the Lord, and He delights in his way.

(Psalm 37:23)

January 17

Today, I declare wisdom and discernment in every decision I make.

If any of you lacks wisdom, you should ask God, who gives generously to all without finding fault.

(James 1:5)

January 18

I prophesy boldness and courage as I step into new opportunities and challenges.

The righteous are as bold as a lion.
(Proverbs 28:1)

January 19

I declare that I am a light to those around me, reflecting God's love and truth.

You are the light of the world. A town built on a hill cannot be hidden.

(Matthew 5:14)

January 20

I declare that God is making a way for me, even where there seems to be no way.

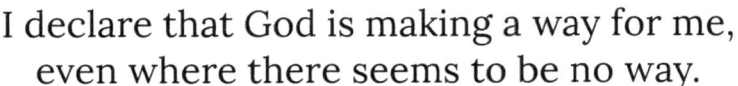

I will even make a way in the wilderness, and rivers in the desert.

(Isaiah 43:19)

January 21

I prophesy new levels of spiritual growth as I draw closer to God today.

Come near to God and he will come near to you.
(James 4:8)

January 22

I declare that today, I walk in joy, regardless of my circumstances, for the joy of the Lord is my strength.

The joy of the Lord is your strength.
(Nehemiah 8:10)

January 23

I declare that I am protected by God's angels as I walk through this day.

For he will command his angels concerning you to guard you in all your ways.

(Psalm 91:11)

January 24

I speak clarity over my thoughts and decisions, knowing God will guide me.

In all your ways submit to him, and he will make your paths straight.

(Proverbs 3:6)

January 25

I declare that my faith will move mountains today, as I trust fully in God.

———•———

Truly I tell you, if you have faith as small as a mustard seed, you can say to this mountain, 'Move from here to there,' and it will move.

(Matthew 17:20)

January 26

I declare that I will walk in humility and grace, knowing God lifts up the humble.

Humble yourselves before the Lord, and he will lift you up.

(James 4:10)

January 27

I prophesy open heavens over my life today, as God pours out His blessings.

Test me in this, says the Lord Almighty, and see if I will not throw open the floodgates of heaven.

(Malachi 3:10)

January 28

Today, I declare that no weapon formed against me shall prosper.

No weapon formed against you shall prosper.
(Isaiah 54:17)

January 29

I declare that I am clothed in God's righteousness and stand firm in His truth.

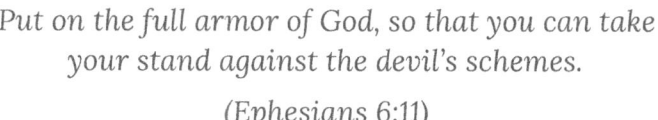

Put on the full armor of God, so that you can take your stand against the devil's schemes.

(Ephesians 6:11)

January 30

I speak life and blessing over my family today, declaring God's protection and favor.

The Lord bless you and keep you; the Lord make his face shine on you and be gracious to you.

(Numbers 6:24-25)

January 31

I declare divine guidance today as I seek God's will in all I do.

The Lord will guide you always; he will satisfy your needs in a sun-scorched land.

(Isaiah 58:11)

February 1

I declare that God is my defender, and I rest in His justice.

The Lord will fight for you; you need only to be still.
(Exodus 14:14)

February 2

Today, I choose to abide in Christ, knowing He is the source of all fruitfulness.

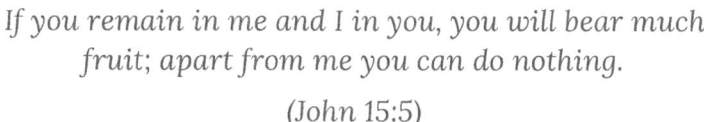

If you remain in me and I in you, you will bear much fruit; apart from me you can do nothing.

(John 15:5)

February 3

I declare that I am seated in heavenly places with Christ, above every power and principality.

And God raised us up with Christ and seated us with him in the heavenly realms in Christ Jesus.

(Ephesians 2:6)

February 4

I declare that my heart and mind are guarded by God's perfect peace.

And the peace of God, which transcends all understanding, will guard your hearts and your minds in Christ Jesus.

(Philippians 4:7)

February 5

I declare that God's promises for my life are yes and amen, and I stand in faith.

For all the promises of God in Him are Yes, and in Him Amen, to the glory of God through us.

(2 Corinthians 1:20)

February 6

Today, I declare that I am a vessel of God's love, showing kindness and compassion.

Be kind and compassionate to one another, forgiving each other, just as in Christ God forgave you.

(Ephesians 4:32)

February 7

I declare victory in every area of spiritual warfare, knowing that God is my strength.

For the weapons of our warfare are not carnal, but mighty through God to the pulling down of strongholds.

(2 Corinthians 10:4)

February 8

I declare that God's light shines brightly in my life, and darkness has no place here.

The light shines in the darkness, and the darkness has not overcome it.

(John 1:5)

February 9

Today, I walk in the freedom that Christ has purchased for me.

It is for freedom that Christ has set us free. Stand firm, then, and do not let yourselves be burdened again by a yoke of slavery.

(Galatians 5:1)

February 10

I prophesy that I will bear much fruit as I abide in the vine of Christ.

———•———

You did not choose me, but I chose you and appointed you so that you might go and bear fruit—fruit that will last.

(John 15:16)

February 11

I declare that God's strength is made perfect in my weakness today.

But he said to me, 'My grace is sufficient for you, for my power is made perfect in weakness.

(2 Corinthians 12:9)

February 12

I declare that God is opening new doors of opportunity and blessing in my life.

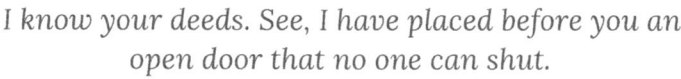

I know your deeds. See, I have placed before you an open door that no one can shut.

(Revelation 3:8)

February 13

I speak resurrection power into every area of my life that feels dead or barren.

The Spirit of God, who raised Jesus from the dead, lives in you.

(Romans 8:11)

February 14

Today, I declare that I am anchored in hope, trusting in the promises of God.

We have this hope as an anchor for the soul, firm and secure.

(Hebrews 6:19)

February 15

I declare that I am rooted and grounded in God's love, and nothing can separate me from it.

And I pray that you, being rooted and established in love, may have power, together with all the Lord's holy people, to grasp how wide and long and high and deep is the love of Christ.

(Ephesians 3:17-18)

February 16

I declare that I will trust in God's timing and wait patiently for His promises to unfold.

———•———

Wait for the Lord; be strong and take heart and wait for the Lord.

(Psalm 27:14)

February 17

I declare that God is healing me from past wounds and restoring my heart.

He heals the brokenhearted and binds up their wounds.

(Psalm 147:3)

February 18

Today, I declare that I am walking in divine favor, and doors of opportunity are opening.

For his anger lasts only a moment, but his favor lasts a lifetime; weeping may stay for the night, but rejoicing comes in the morning.

(Psalm 30:5)

February 19

I declare that I am a child of God, and I walk in the inheritance of His promises.

The Spirit himself testifies with our spirit that we are God's children. Now if we are children, then we are heirs—heirs of God and co-heirs with Christ.

(Romans 8:16-17)

February 20

I declare that God's goodness and mercy follow me all the days of my life.

Surely your goodness and love will follow me all the days of my life, and I will dwell in the house of the Lord forever.

(Psalm 23:6)

February 21

I declare that I will seek first the kingdom of God, and He will supply all my needs.

But seek first his kingdom and his righteousness, and all these things will be given to you as well.

(Matthew 6:33)

February 22

I declare that God is my refuge and strength, an ever-present help in times of trouble.

God is our refuge and strength, an ever-present help in trouble.

(Psalm 46:1)

February 23

I declare that I am walking in the joy of the Lord, which is my strength.

Do not grieve, for the joy of the Lord is your strength.

(Nehemiah 8:10)

February 24

I declare that God is transforming me by renewing my mind, and I am being made new.

Do not conform to the pattern of this world, but be transformed by the renewing of your mind.

(Romans 12:2)

February 25

Today, I declare that God's protection surrounds me, and no harm will come near my dwelling.

Because you have made the Lord your dwelling place—the Most High, who is my refuge—no evil shall be allowed to befall you, no plague come near your tent.

(Psalm 91:9-10)

February 26

I declare that I am a new creation in Christ, and the old has passed away.

Therefore, if anyone is in Christ, the new creation has come: The old has gone, the new is here!

(2 Corinthians 5:17)

February 27

I declare that God will give me beauty for ashes, and joy for my mourning.

To comfort all who mourn, and provide for those who grieve in Zion— to bestow on them a crown of beauty instead of ashes, the oil of joy instead of mourning.

(Isaiah 61:3)

February 28

I declare that I am walking in God's truth, and His word is a lamp to my feet.

Your word is a lamp to my feet and a light to my path.

(Psalm 119:105)

March 1

I declare that I am fearlessly and wonderfully made, and God's plans for me are good.

For I know the plans I have for you, declares the Lord, plans for welfare and not for evil, to give you a future and a hope.

(Jeremiah 29:11)

March 2

I declare that God will turn my mourning into dancing and fill my heart with joy.

You have turned my mourning into joyful dancing. You have taken away my clothes of mourning and clothed me with joy.

(Psalm 30:11)

March 3

I declare that God is my provider, and I will lack nothing I need.

And my God will meet all your needs according to the riches of his glory in Christ Jesus.

(Philippians 4:19)

March 4

I declare that God is with me through the storm, and I will not be shaken.

When you pass through the waters, I will be with you; and when you pass through the rivers, they will not sweep over you.

(Isaiah 43:2)

March 5

I declare that I am filled with the Holy Spirit, and I walk in power and authority.

But you will receive power when the Holy Spirit comes on you; and you will be my witnesses.

(Acts 1:8)

March 6

I declare that I will experience God's peace that surpasses all understanding.

And the peace of God, which transcends all understanding, will guard your hearts and your minds in Christ Jesus.

(Philippians 4:7)

March 7

I declare that I am led by the Holy Spirit in every decision I make today.

For those who are led by the Spirit of God are the children of God.

(Romans 8:14)

March 8

I declare that I am strong and courageous, for God goes before me.

Be strong and courageous. Do not be afraid; do not be discouraged, for the Lord your God will be with you wherever you go.

(Joshua 1:9)

March 9

I declare that God is my helper, and I will not be afraid.

The Lord is my helper; I will not be afraid. What can mere mortals do to me?

(Hebrews 13:6)

March 10

I declare that I will walk by faith, not by sight, trusting in God's promises.

For we live by faith, not by sight.
(2 Corinthians 5:7)

March 11

I declare that God is my comforter, and His presence brings me peace.

Blessed are those who mourn, for they will be comforted.

(Matthew 5:4)

March 12

I declare that I will stand firm in the truth of God's word, no matter what comes my way.

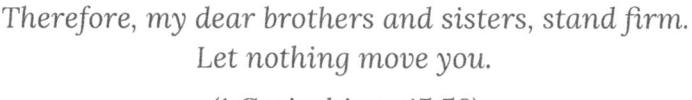

Therefore, my dear brothers and sisters, stand firm. Let nothing move you.

(1 Corinthians 15:58)

March 12

I declare that God is transforming my life, and His plans for me are good.

The Lord will fulfill his purpose for me; your steadfast love, O Lord, endures forever.

(Psalm 138:8)

March 13

I declare that today, I will sow seeds of righteousness and reap a harvest of blessing.

Let us not become weary in doing good, for at the proper time we will reap a harvest if we do not give up.

(Galatians 6:9)

March 14

I declare that God is my protector, and I take refuge in His name.

The name of the Lord is a fortified tower; the righteous run to it and are safe.

(Proverbs 18:10)

March 15

I declare that I will be still and know that He is God, trusting Him in all things.

"Be still, and know that I am God."
(Psalm 46:10)

March 16

I declare that God is working behind the scenes, even when I don't see it.

My Father is always at his work to this very day, and I too am working.

(John 5:17)

March 17

I declare that I am walking in God's wisdom, and He will make my paths straight.

Trust in the Lord with all your heart and lean not on your own understanding; in all your ways submit to him, and he will make your paths straight.

(Proverbs 3:5-6)

March 18

I declare that today, I will see God's goodness in the land of the living.

I remain confident of this: I will see the goodness of the Lord in the land of the living.

(Psalm 27:13)

March 19

I declare that God is doing a new thing in my life, and I am ready to receive it.

---

*Forget the former things; do not dwell on the past.
See, I am doing a new thing!*
(Isaiah 43:18-19)

March 20

I declare that God's grace is sufficient for me in all things today.

But he said to me, My grace is sufficient for you, for my power is made perfect in weakness.

(2 Corinthians 12:9)

March 21

I declare that God is able to do immeasurably more than I ask or imagine.

Now to him who is able to do immeasurably more than all we ask or imagine, according to his power that is at work within us.

(Ephesians 3:20)

March 22

I declare that God is renewing my strength, and I will soar on wings like eagles.

But those who hope in the Lord will renew their strength. They will soar on wings like eagles.

(Isaiah 40:31)

March 23

I declare that God is my refuge and my fortress, and I trust in Him.

I will say of the Lord, 'He is my refuge and my fortress, my God, in whom I trust.
(Psalm 91:2)

March 24

I declare that I am filled with God's perfect love, which drives out all fear.

There is no fear in love. But perfect love drives out fear.

(1 John 4:18)

March 25

I declare that I am fruitful in every good work, and I am growing in the knowledge of God.

So that you may live a life worthy of the Lord and please him in every way: bearing fruit in every good work, growing in the knowledge of God.

(Colossians 1:10)

March 26

I declare that God's word is alive in me, and it will accomplish His purpose.

So is my word that goes out from my mouth: It will not return to me empty, but will accomplish what I desire and achieve the purpose for which I sent it.

(Isaiah 55:11)

March 27

I declare that I will not grow weary, for God will strengthen and uphold me.

So do not fear, for I am with you; do not be dismayed, for I am your God. I will strengthen you and help you.

(Isaiah 41:10)

March 28

I declare that God's love and faithfulness will never leave me.

Because of the Lord's great love we are not consumed, for his compassions never fail. They are new every morning.

(Lamentations 3:22-23)

March 29

I declare that I will not be anxious, but I will trust God with all my heart.

Do not be anxious about anything, but in every situation, by prayer and petition, with thanksgiving, present your requests to God.

(Philippians 4:6)

March 30

I declare that I will walk in God's purpose for my life and fulfill His plans.

The Lord will fulfill his purpose for me; your steadfast love, O Lord, endures forever.

(Psalm 138:8)

March 31

I declare that God is my provider, and I will experience His abundant provision today.

The Lord is my shepherd; I lack nothing.
(Psalm 23:1)

April 1

I declare that I am walking in divine health—body, soul, and spirit are made whole.

Dear friend, I pray that you may enjoy good health and that all may go well with you, even as your soul is getting along well.

(3 John 1:2)

April 2

I declare that God is blessing the work of my hands and increasing my resources.

The Lord will open the heavens, the storehouse of his bounty, to send rain on your land in season and to bless all the work of your hands.

(Deuteronomy 28:12)

April 3

I declare that I will prosper in all things, even as my soul prospers.

Beloved, I wish above all things that you may prosper and be in health, even as your soul prospers.

(3 John 1:2)

April 4

I declare that my body is a temple of the Holy Spirit, and I honor God with it.

Do you not know that your bodies are temples of the Holy Spirit, who is in you, whom you have received from God?

(1 Corinthians 6:19)

April 5

I declare that God will supply all my needs according to His riches in glory.

───•───

And my God will meet all your needs according to the riches of his glory in Christ Jesus.

(Philippians 4:19)

April 6

I declare that I am blessed in my coming and my going, and favor surrounds me.

You will be blessed when you come in and blessed when you go out.

(Deuteronomy 28:6)

April 7

I declare that God is releasing supernatural abundance and overflow in my life.

Give, and it will be given to you. A good measure, pressed down, shaken together and running over, will be poured into your lap.

(Luke 6:38)

April 8

I declare that I walk in divine wisdom and stewardship over my finances.

The plans of the diligent lead surely to abundance, but everyone who is hasty comes only to poverty.

(Proverbs 21:5)

April 9

I declare that I am blessed to be a blessing, and I will sow generously into God's kingdom.

You will be enriched in every way so that you can be generous on every occasion, and through us your generosity will result in thanksgiving to God.

(2 Corinthians 9:11)

April 10

I declare that my soul finds rest in God, and He restores my spirit.

He restores my soul; He leads me in the paths of righteousness for His name's sake.

(Psalm 23:3)

April 11

I declare that I will flourish like a tree planted by streams of living water.

That person is like a tree planted by streams of water, which yields its fruit in season and whose leaf does not wither—whatever they do prospers.

(Psalm 1:3)

April 12

I declare that God is bringing healing to my body, soul, and spirit.

But I will restore you to health and heal your wounds, declares the Lord.

(Jeremiah 30:17)

April 13

I declare that I am fruitful and multiplying in every area of my life.

Be fruitful and multiply; fill the earth and subdue it.
(Genesis 1:28)

April 14

I declare that I am walking in supernatural health and divine strength today.

But those who hope in the Lord will renew their strength. They will soar on wings like eagles.

(Isaiah 40:31)

April 15

I declare that I am blessed in all areas of my life, and I will see God's abundance.

The blessing of the Lord brings wealth, without painful toil for it.
(Proverbs 10:22)

April 16

I declare that I am a good steward of the resources God has entrusted to me.

Who then is the faithful and wise servant, whom the master has put in charge of the servants in his household to give them their food at the proper time?

(Matthew 24:45)

April 17

I declare that God is healing and restoring broken areas in my life.

He heals the brokenhearted and binds up their wounds.

(Psalm 147:3)

April 18

I declare that I am surrounded by God's favor, and I am blessed to be a blessing.

Surely, Lord, you bless the righteous; you surround them with your favor as with a shield.

(Psalm 5:12)

April 19

I declare that God is giving me wisdom and revelation to manage my finances well.

If any of you lacks wisdom, you should ask God, who gives generously to all without finding fault, and it will be given to you.

(James 1:5)

April 20

I declare that God is making all grace abound to me, so I may abound in every good work.

And God is able to bless you abundantly, so that in all things at all times, having all that you need, you will abound in every good work.

(2 Corinthians 9:8)

April 21

I declare that I will walk in health and wholeness, and God is renewing my strength.

Worship the Lord your God, and his blessing will be on your food and water. I will take away sickness from among you.
(Exodus 23:25)

April 22

I declare that God is releasing financial blessings and increase into my life.

———•———

The Lord will grant you abundant prosperity—in the fruit of your womb, the young of your livestock and the crops of your ground—in the land he swore to your ancestors to give you.

(Deuteronomy 28:11)

April 23

I declare that God is opening my spiritual eyes to see dreams and visions from Him.

In the last days, God says, I will pour out my Spirit on all people. Your sons and daughters will prophesy, your young men will see visions, your old men will dream dreams.

(Acts 2:17)

April 24

I declare that I will walk in signs and wonders, demonstrating the power of God's Spirit.

God also testified to it by signs, wonders and various miracles, and by gifts of the Holy Spirit distributed according to his will.

(Hebrews 2:4)

April 25

I declare that I will hear God's voice clearly and receive divine revelation for my life.

My sheep listen to my voice; I know them, and they follow me.

(John 10:27)

April 26

I declare that I am a vessel for God's power, and I will move in miracles and wonders.

Truly I tell you, whoever believes in me will do the works I have been doing, and they will do even greater things than these.

(John 14:12)

April 27

I declare that I will receive heavenly downloads of wisdom and understanding in dreams.

He speaks in dreams, in visions of the night, when deep sleep falls on people as they lie in their beds.

(Job 33:15)

April 28

I declare that I will move in supernatural faith, releasing signs and wonders wherever I go.

———•———

By faith, the apostles performed many signs and wonders among the people.

(Acts 5:12)

April 29

I declare that God is revealing deep mysteries and secrets to me by His Spirit.

He reveals deep and hidden things; He knows what lies in darkness, and light dwells with Him.

(Daniel 2:22)

April 30

I declare that I will receive visions that reveal God's plans and purposes.

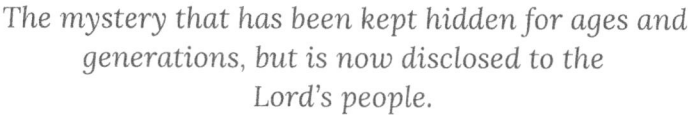

The mystery that has been kept hidden for ages and generations, but is now disclosed to the Lord's people.

(Colossians 1:26)

May 1

I declare that I will operate in spiritual gifts, including prophecy, healing, and miracles.

Now to each one the manifestation of the Spirit is given for the common good.

(1 Corinthians 12:7)

May 2

I declare that God is unlocking fresh revelation and insights as I spend time in His presence.

Call to me and I will answer you and tell you great and unsearchable things you do not know.

(Jeremiah 33:3)

May 3

I declare that I am filled with the Spirit of wisdom and revelation, so I may know God more.

I keep asking that the God of our Lord Jesus Christ, the glorious Father, may give you the Spirit of wisdom and revelation, so that you may know him better.

(Ephesians 1:17)

May 4

I declare that God will give me dreams that unlock heavenly strategies for my life.

But when he, the Spirit of truth, comes, he will guide you into all the truth. He will not speak on his own; he will speak only what he hears, and he will tell you what is yet to come.

(John 16:13)

May 5

I declare that I am walking in the power and authority that Jesus has given me, to do greater works.

He called the twelve together and gave them power and authority over all demons and to cure diseases.

(Luke 9:1)

May 6

I declare that I will receive divine understanding and prophetic insight to speak God's truth.

For the Lord God does nothing without revealing his secret to his servants the prophets.

(Amos 3:7)

May 7

I declare that the Holy Spirit is giving me dreams and visions to reveal His plans and purposes.

Your young men will see visions, your old men will dream dreams.

(Joel 2:28)

May 8

I declare that I will experience supernatural signs, miracles, and wonders in my life.

I will show wonders in the heavens and on the earth.

(Joel 2:30)

May 9

I declare that God will use me to bring healing and deliverance to others through His power.

Heal the sick, raise the dead, cleanse those who have leprosy, drive out demons. Freely you have received; freely give.

(Matthew 10:8)

May 10

I declare that I am growing in the knowledge of God and receiving supernatural revelation.

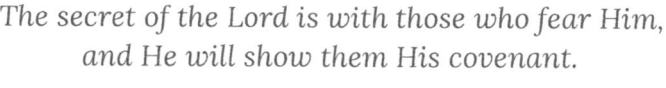

The secret of the Lord is with those who fear Him, and He will show them His covenant.

(Psalm 25:14)

May 11

I declare that I am open to God's supernatural guidance through dreams, visions, and signs.

After this I will pour out my Spirit on all humanity. Your sons and daughters will prophesy, your old men will have prophetic dreams, your young men will see visions.

(Joel 2:28)

May 11

I declare that the Holy Spirit is stirring up the gifts within me to do the works of God.

Do not neglect the spiritual gift you received.
(1 Timothy 4:14)

May 12

I declare that God is increasing my capacity to receive dreams and visions from Him.

For God speaks again and again, though people do not recognize it. He speaks in dreams, in visions of the night.

(Job 33:14-15)

May 13

I declare that I am stepping into a new level of revelation and spiritual understanding.

The Spirit searches all things, even the deep things of God.

(1 Corinthians 2:10)

May 14

I declare that I will not fear the future, for God is with me and His plans are good.

For I know the plans I have for you, declares the Lord, plans to prosper you and not to harm you, plans to give you a hope and a future.

(Jeremiah 29:11)

May 15

I declare that I am filled with hope and confidence, trusting God for what's to come.

———•———

But those who hope in the Lord will renew their strength. They will soar on wings like eagles.
(Isaiah 40:31)

May 16

I declare that I will not be discouraged, for God is working all things for my good.

And we know that in all things God works for the good of those who love him, who have been called according to his purpose.

(Romans 8:28)

May 17

I declare that God is my refuge and strength, and I will not fear what lies ahead.

God is our refuge and strength, an ever-present help in trouble. Therefore we will not fear.

(Psalm 46:1-2)

May 18

I declare that I have hope for the future because God's promises are unshakable.

Let us hold unswervingly to the hope we profess, for he who promised is faithful.

(Hebrews 10:23)

May 19

I declare that God's peace guards my heart, and I will not be anxious about the future.

Do not be anxious about anything, but in every situation, by prayer and petition, with thanksgiving, present your requests to God.

(Philippians 4:6)

May 20

I declare that God is opening new doors of opportunity for me, and I will walk through them with boldness.

See, I have placed before you an open door that no one can shut.

(Revelation 3:8)

May 21

I declare that I will not fear, for God's perfect love casts out all fear.

There is no fear in love. But perfect love drives out fear.

(1 John 4:18)

May 22

I declare that God will turn every challenge into a testimony of His faithfulness.

You intended to harm me, but God intended it for good to accomplish what is now being done, the saving of many lives.

(Genesis 50:20)

May 23

I declare that God is bringing restoration and hope to every area of my life.

I will repay you for the years the locusts have eaten.
(Joel 2:25)

May 24

I declare that I will not fear the unknown, for God goes before me and prepares the way.

The Lord himself goes before you and will be with you; he will never leave you nor forsake you. Do not be afraid; do not be discouraged.

(Deuteronomy 31:8)

May 25

I declare that my future is filled with hope because God's faithfulness never ends.

Because of the Lord's great love we are not consumed, for his compassions never fail. They are new every morning; great is your faithfulness.

(Lamentations 3:22-23)

May 26

I declare that I will stand firm in faith, knowing that God's timing is perfect.

For the vision is yet for an appointed time; but at the end it shall speak, and not lie: though it tarry, wait for it; because it will surely come, it will not tarry.

(Habakkuk 2:3)

May 27

I declare that I will trust God's plans for my life, even when I don't understand them.

Trust in the Lord with all your heart and lean not on your own understanding.

(Proverbs 3:5)

May 28

I declare that I will not grow weary in doing good, for God will bring a harvest in His time.

Let us not become weary in doing good, for at the proper time we will reap a harvest if we do not give up.

(Galatians 6:9)

May 29

I declare that God's word is a light to my path, and He will guide me into my future.

Your word is a lamp to my feet and a light to my path.

(Psalm 119:105)

May 30

I declare that I will see the goodness of God in my life, and my hope is secure in Him.

I remain confident of this: I will see the goodness of the Lord in the land of the living.

(Psalm 27:13)

May 31

I am confident that God began a good work within me, and He will continue to do so throughout my whole life on this earth.

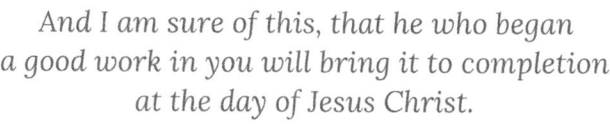

And I am sure of this, that he who began a good work in you will bring it to completion at the day of Jesus Christ.

(Philippians 1:6)

June 1

I declare that God is working behind the scenes, preparing great things for my future.

No eye has seen, no ear has heard, and no human mind has conceived the things God has prepared for those who love him.

(1 Corinthians 2:9)

June 2

I declare that I am filled with courage and hope, for God's promises never fail.

———•———

Not one of all the Lord's good promises to Israel failed; every one was fulfilled.

(Joshua 21:45)

June 3

I declare that God is taking me from glory to glory, and my future is bright in Him.

And we all, who with unveiled faces contemplate the Lord's glory, are being transformed into his image with ever-increasing glory.

(2 Corinthians 3:18)

June 4

I declare that the Spirit of God is revealing the future to me, and I will walk in His plans.

But when he, the Spirit of truth, comes, he will guide you into all the truth. He will tell you what is yet to come.

(John 16:13)

June 5

I declare that I will not be dismayed by challenges, for God is fighting my battles.

Do not be afraid or discouraged because of this vast army. For the battle is not yours, but God's."

(2 Chronicles 20:15)

June 6

I declare that I will move forward in faith, knowing God's plans are greater than my fears.

For God has not given us a spirit of fear, but of power and of love and of a sound mind.

(2 Timothy 1:7)

June 7

I declare that God is my hope and my strength, and I will not be shaken.

Truly he is my rock and my salvation; he is my fortress, I will not be shaken.

(Psalm 62:6)

June 8

I declare that God is restoring everything that has been lost and bringing hope to my future.

And the God of all grace, who called you to his eternal glory in Christ, after you have suffered a little while, will himself restore you and make you strong, firm and steadfast.

(1 Peter 5:10)

June 9

I declare that God is pouring out His Spirit on me, and I will see visions and dream dreams.

In the last days, God says, I will pour out my Spirit on all people. Your sons and daughters will prophesy, your young men will see visions, your old men will dream dreams.

(Acts 2:17)

June 10

I declare that I will not fear tomorrow, for God holds my future in His hands.

Therefore do not worry about tomorrow, for tomorrow will worry about itself. Each day has enough trouble of its own.

(Matthew 6:34)

June 11

I declare that I will experience supernatural provision and abundance from God.

And God is able to bless you abundantly, so that in all things at all times, having all that you need, you will abound in every good work.

(2 Corinthians 9:8)

June 12

I declare that I will see God's miracles and signs in my life, for nothing is impossible with Him.

With man this is impossible, but with God all things are possible.

(Matthew 19:26)

June 13

I declare that I will walk in divine health, and every part of my being is restored.

He sent out his word and healed them; he rescued them from the grave.

(Psalm 107:20)

June 14

I declare that God is giving me fresh revelation and insight to walk in His will.

Call to me and I will answer you and tell you great and unsearchable things you do not know.

(Jeremiah 33:3)

June 15

I declare that I will not be discouraged, for God is working out His perfect plan for me.

And we know that in all things God works for the good of those who love him, who have been called according to his purpose.

(Romans 8:28)

June 16

I declare that God's abundance flows through my life, and I will see financial blessings.

You will be enriched in every way so that you can be generous on every occasion.

(2 Corinthians 9:11)

June 17

I declare that I will hear the voice of God clearly, and He will direct my steps.

Whether you turn to the right or to the left, your ears will hear a voice behind you, saying, 'This is the way; walk in it.

(Isaiah 30:21)

June 18

I declare that my hope is in God alone, and He will not fail me.

We wait in hope for the Lord; he is our help and our shield.

(Psalm 33:20)

June 19

I declare that I will move in the power of the Holy Spirit and witness miracles in my life.

But you will receive power when the Holy Spirit comes on you; and you will be my witnesses.

(Acts 1:8)

June 20

I declare that God is renewing my strength, and I will soar on wings like eagles.

But those who hope in the Lord will renew their strength. They will soar on wings like eagles.

(Isaiah 40:31)

June 21

I declare that I am walking in God's favor, and His blessings will overtake me.

All these blessings will come on you and accompany you if you obey the Lord your God.

(Deuteronomy 28:2)

June 22

I declare that God is increasing my capacity to receive dreams, visions, and revelations.

I will pour out my Spirit on all people. Your sons and daughters will prophesy, your young men will see visions, your old men will dream dreams.

(Joel 2:28)

June 23

I declare that I will not fear the future, for God has already made a way for me.

The Lord will fight for you; you need only to be still.
(Exodus 14:14)

June 24

I declare that God is healing every part of me—body, soul, and spirit.

Dear friend, I pray that you may enjoy good health and that all may go well with you, even as your soul is getting along well.

(3 John 1:2)

June 25

I declare that I will receive divine wisdom and knowledge to steward God's revelations.

If any of you lacks wisdom, you should ask God, who gives generously to all without finding fault, and it will be given to you.

(James 1:5)

June 26

I declare that I will see God's goodness in the land of the living, and my hope is secure.

I remain confident of this: I will see the goodness of the Lord in the land of the living.
(Psalm 27:13)

June 27

I declare that God is increasing my faith to move mountains and see miracles unfold.

Truly I tell you, if you have faith as small as a mustard seed, you can say to this mountain, 'Move from here to there,' and it will move.

(Matthew 17:20)

June 28

I declare that I am free from fear and anxiety because God's perfect love casts out all fear.

There is no fear in love. But perfect love drives out fear.

(1 John 4:18)

June 29

I declare that God is giving me the strength and perseverance to fulfill my calling.

I can do all this through him who gives me strength.
(Philippians 4:13)

June 30

I declare that I will see dreams and visions that reveal God's purposes for my life.

For God speaks again and again, though people do not recognize it. He speaks in dreams, in visions of the night.

(Job 33:14-15)

July 1

I declare that God is making a way where there seems to be no way, and I will trust Him.

I will even make a way in the wilderness and rivers in the desert.

(Isaiah 43:19)

July 2

I declare that I am blessed in all that I do, and God's favor surrounds me like a shield.

Surely, Lord, you bless the righteous; you surround them with your favor as with a shield.

(Psalm 5:12)

July 3

I declare that I will see signs and wonders in my life, confirming the word of God.

Then the disciples went out and preached everywhere, and the Lord worked with them and confirmed his word by the signs that accompanied it.

(Mark 16:20)

July 4

I declare that God is my refuge and fortress, and I will not be afraid of the future.

He is my refuge and my fortress, my God, in whom I trust.

(Psalm 91:2)

July 5

I declare that God is leading me into deeper revelations and understanding of His will.

The Spirit searches all things, even the deep things of God.

(1 Corinthians 2:10)

July 6

I declare that I will receive prophetic dreams and visions that reveal God's plans.

In the last days, God says, I will pour out my Spirit on all people. Your sons and daughters will prophesy, your young men will see visions.

(Acts 2:17)

July 7

I declare that I will not be discouraged, for God is renewing my hope and strength.

But those who hope in the Lord will renew their strength. They will soar on wings like eagles.

(Isaiah 40:31)

July 8

I declare that signs will accompany me because I believe, and in the name of Jesus I will drive out any demonic attacks or influence that tries to come against me!

These signs will accompany those who believe: In my name they will drive out demons; they will speak in new tongues.

(Mark 16:17)

July 9

I declare that I will see the supernatural manifest in my life as I walk in faith.

Now faith is confidence in what we hope for and assurance about what we do not see.

(Hebrews 11:1)

July 10

I declare that God is releasing dreams and visions to guide me into His divine purposes.

He speaks in dreams, in visions of the night, when deep sleep falls on people as they lie in their beds.

(Job 33:15)

July 11

I declare that I will experience miraculous breakthroughs as I trust in God's timing.

For nothing will be impossible with God.
(Luke 1:37)

July 12

I declare that I am walking in divine abundance, and God is blessing the work of my hands.

The Lord will open the heavens, the storehouse of his bounty, to send rain on your land in season and to bless all the work of your hands.

(Deuteronomy 28:12)

July 13

I declare that I will not be afraid, for God is my protector and my strong tower.

The Lord is my light and my salvation—whom shall I fear? The Lord is the stronghold of my life—of whom shall I be afraid?

(Psalm 27:1)

July 14

I declare that God's healing power is at work in my body, soul, and spirit.

He heals the brokenhearted and binds up their wounds.

(Psalm 147:3)

July 15

I declare that I am growing in prophetic insight and receiving fresh revelation from God.

For the Lord God does nothing without revealing his secret to his servants the prophets.

(Amos 3:7)

July 16

I declare that I will see dreams and visions that reveal God's plans and purposes.

The Spirit of the Lord will come upon you in power, and you will prophesy with them; and you will be changed into a different person.

(1 Samuel 10:6)

July 17

I declare that God is releasing supernatural provision into my life, and I will not lack.

And my God will meet all your needs according to the riches of his glory in Christ Jesus.

(Philippians 4:19)

July 18

I declare that God is guiding me with His wisdom, and I will make decisions led by His Spirit.

For the Lord gives wisdom; from his mouth come knowledge and understanding.

(Proverbs 2:6)

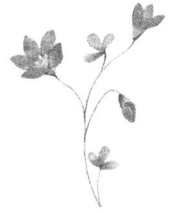

July 19

I declare that I will see miracles in my life and the lives of those around me as I walk in faith.

Jesus said to her, 'Did I not tell you that if you believe, you will see the glory of God?

(John 11:40)

July 20

I declare that I will overcome every obstacle, for God goes before me and makes a way.

I will go before you and make the crooked places straight.

(Isaiah 45:2)

July 21

I declare that I will move in signs and wonders, releasing the power of God wherever I go.

The apostles performed many signs and wonders among the people."
(Acts 5:12)

July 22

I declare that I am walking in divine health, and every part of me is being restored.

But I will restore you to health and heal your wounds, declares the Lord.

(Jeremiah 30:17)

July 23

I declare that I will hear God's voice clearly, and I will follow His direction for my life.

Whether you turn to the right or to the left, your ears will hear a voice behind you, saying, 'This is the way; walk in it.

(Isaiah 30:21)

July 24

I declare that I am filled with supernatural courage and boldness to step into my destiny.

The righteous are as bold as a lion.

(Proverbs 28:1)

July 25

I declare that God is opening the heavens over me and releasing supernatural blessings.

Bring the whole tithe into the storehouse, that there may be food in my house. Test me in this, says the Lord Almighty, and see if I will not throw open the floodgates of heaven.

(Malachi 3:10)

July 26

I declare that I will not be afraid of the unknown, for God is my guide and my protector.

Even though I walk through the darkest valley, I will fear no evil, for you are with me.
(Psalm 23:4)

July 27

I declare that God is revealing deep mysteries and heavenly strategies to me in dreams and visions.

He reveals deep and hidden things; he knows what lies in darkness, and light dwells with him.

(Daniel 2:22)

July 28

I declare that God is renewing my hope and strength, and I will not be discouraged.

But those who hope in the Lord will renew their strength. They will soar on wings like eagles.

(Isaiah 40:31)

July 29

I declare that I will receive revelation that unlocks new levels of faith and spiritual understanding.

Call to me and I will answer you and tell you great and unsearchable things you do not know.

(Jeremiah 33:3)

July 30

I declare that God is releasing supernatural protection over me and my family.

He will cover you with his feathers, and under his wings you will find refuge.

(Psalm 91:4)

July 31

I declare that I will see God's promises fulfilled in my life, for His word never fails.

Not one of all the Lord's good promises to Israel failed; every one was fulfilled.

(Joshua 21:45)

August 1

I declare that God is opening doors that no man can shut, and I will walk through them with faith.

See, I have placed before you an open door that no one can shut.

(Revelation 3:8)

August 2

I declare that God is releasing new dreams and visions to direct me into His perfect will.

Your sons and daughters will prophesy, your young men will see visions, your old men will dream dreams.

(Acts 2:17)

August 3

I declare that God is restoring everything that has been lost and turning it into a blessing.

I will repay you for the years the locusts have eaten.
(Joel 2:25)

August 4

I declare that I will not fear the future, for God is already there, and His plans are good.

For I know the plans I have for you, declares the Lord, plans to prosper you and not to harm you, plans to give you a hope and a future.

(Jeremiah 29:11)

August 5

I declare that I am filled with faith and hope, and I will walk in the promises of God.

Let us hold unswervingly to the hope we profess, for he who promised is faithful.

(Hebrews 10:23)

August 6

I declare that God is giving me supernatural wisdom to navigate every situation with clarity.

If any of you lacks wisdom, you should ask God, who gives generously to all without finding fault.

(James 1:5)

August 7

I declare that I will move in signs, wonders, and miracles, demonstrating God's power.

For the kingdom of God is not a matter of talk but of power.

(1 Corinthians 4:20)

August 8

I declare that God is expanding my faith to believe for the impossible and to see His miracles.

Truly I tell you, if you have faith and do not doubt, you can say to this mountain, 'Go, throw yourself into the sea,' and it will be done.

(Matthew 21:21)

August 9

I declare that I am walking in divine health, and no weapon formed against my body will prosper.

No weapon formed against you shall prosper, and you will refute every tongue that accuses you.

(Isaiah 54:17)

August 10

I declare that God is making me fruitful, and I will multiply in every area of my life.

Be fruitful and increase in number; fill the earth and subdue it.

(Genesis 1:28)

August 11

I declare that I will receive prophetic dreams that reveal God's plans for my *future*.

God speaks again and again, though people do not recognize it. He speaks in dreams, in visions of the night.

(Job 33:14-15)

August 12

I declare that God is pouring out His Spirit on me, and I will prophesy and walk in His power.

I will pour out my Spirit on all people. Your sons and daughters will prophesy.

(Joel 2:28)

August 13

I declare that I am victorious in every battle because the Lord fights for me.

The Lord will fight for you; you need only to be still.
(Exodus 14:14)

August 14

I declare that I will move forward in faith, and I will not shrink back in fear.

But my righteous one will live by faith. And I take no pleasure in the one who shrinks back.

(Hebrews 10:38)

August 15

I declare that God is blessing me with creativity and divine ideas to accomplish His will.

But it is the spirit in a person, the breath of the Almighty, that gives them understanding.

(Job 32:8)

August 16

I declare that I will experience supernatural provision and favor in every area of my life.

The blessing of the Lord brings wealth, without painful toil for it.

(Proverbs 10:22)

August 17

I declare that I will receive new revelations from God as I seek His face in prayer.

The secret of the Lord is with those who fear Him, and He will show them His covenant.

(Psalm 25:14)

August 18

I declare that I am covered by God's protection, and no harm will come near me.

Because you have made the Lord your dwelling place—the Most High, who is my refuge—no evil shall be allowed to befall you.

(Psalm 91:9-10)

August 19

I declare that I will not grow weary in doing good, for I will see a harvest in due season.

Let us not become weary in doing good, for at the proper time we will reap a harvest if we do not give up.

(Galatians 6:9)

August 20

I declare that God's light will shine through me, and I will bring hope and encouragement to others.

You are the light of the world. A town built on a hill cannot be hidden.

(Matthew 5:14)

August 21

I declare that God is opening my spiritual eyes to see His purpose and plans for me.

Open my eyes that I may see wonderful things in your law.

(Psalm 119:18)

August 22

I declare that I will not fear the future, for God's plans for me are greater than I can imagine.

No eye has seen, no ear has heard, no mind has conceived what God has prepared for those who love him.

(1 Corinthians 2:9)

August 23

I declare that God is releasing supernatural breakthroughs in my finances and resources.

The Lord will open the heavens, the storehouse of his bounty, to send rain on your land in season.

(Deuteronomy 28:12)

August 24

I declare that I will move in boldness and authority, demonstrating the power of the Holy Spirit.

For the kingdom of God is not a matter of talk but of power.

(1 Corinthians 4:20)

August 25

I declare that God is healing me from past wounds and restoring my heart.

He heals the brokenhearted and binds up their wounds.

(Psalm 147:3)

August 26

I declare that I will receive divine strategies and wisdom to fulfill my calling.

If any of you lacks wisdom, you should ask God, who gives generously to all without finding fault.

(James 1:5)

August 27

I declare that I am walking in God's favor, and every step I take is blessed.

Surely, Lord, you bless the righteous; you surround them with your favor as with a shield.

(Psalm 5:12)

August 28

I declare that I will see dreams and visions that reveal God's plans and guide my steps.

I will pour out my Spirit on all people. Your sons and daughters will prophesy, your young men will see visions.

(Joel 2:28)

August 29

I declare that God is leading me into new seasons of growth, blessing, and opportunity.

The righteous will flourish like a palm tree, they will grow like a cedar of Lebanon.

(Psalm 92:12)

August 30

I declare that I am a vessel of God's healing power, and I will bring His peace to others.

Heal the sick, raise the dead, cleanse those who have leprosy, drive out demons. Freely you have received; freely give.

(Matthew 10:8)

August 31

I declare God's peace reigns over my heart, and I will not allow fear to take root.

Peace I leave with you; my peace I give you. I do not give to you as the world gives. Do not let your hearts be troubled and do not be afraid.

(John 14:27)

September 1

I declare that God's abundance flows in my life, and I will be generous in every season.

You will be enriched in every way so that you can be generous on every occasion.

(2 Corinthians 9:11)

September 2

I declare that I will not fear any challenge, for God is with me and strengthens me.

So do not fear, for I am with you; do not be dismayed, for I am your God. I will strengthen you and help you.

(Isaiah 41:10)

September 3

I declare that God is releasing new levels of revelation, and I will walk in His truth.

The Spirit of truth will guide you into all truth.
(John 16:13)

September 4

I declare that I am more than a conqueror in Christ, and nothing can separate me from His love.

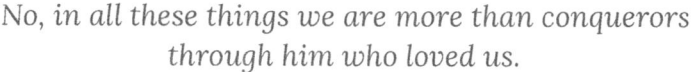

No, in all these things we are more than conquerors through him who loved us.

(Romans 8:37)

September 5

I declare that I am walking in divine wisdom, and my steps are ordered by the Lord.

The steps of a good man are ordered by the Lord.
(Psalm 37:23)

September 6

I declare that God's peace guards my heart and mind, and I will not be anxious about anything.

And the peace of God, which transcends all understanding, will guard your hearts and your minds in Christ Jesus.

(Philippians 4:7)

September 7

I declare that I am growing in spiritual maturity, and God is revealing deeper truths to me.

The Spirit searches all things, even the deep things of God.

(1 Corinthians 2:10)

September 8

I declare that I am free from fear because God's perfect love casts out all fear.

There is no fear in love. But perfect love drives out fear.

(1 John 4:18)

September 9

I declare that God's peace guards my heart, and I will rest in His promises.

You will keep in perfect peace those whose minds are steadfast, because they trust in you.

(Isaiah 26:3)

September 10

I declare that I am not anxious about anything, for God is in control of my life.

Do not be anxious about anything, but in every situation, by prayer and petition, with thanksgiving, present your requests to God.

(Philippians 4:6)

September 11

I declare that God's peace, which surpasses understanding, fills my heart and mind.

And the peace of God, which transcends all understanding, will guard your hearts and your minds in Christ Jesus.

(Philippians 4:7)

September 12

I declare that I will fear no evil, for God is with me and He protects me.

Even though I walk through the darkest valley, I will fear no evil, for you are with me; your rod and your staff, they comfort me.

(Psalm 23:4)

September 13

I declare that I am free from fear of the future, for God has a good plan for my life.

For I know the plans I have for you, declares the Lord, plans to prosper you and not to harm you, plans to give you hope and a future.

(Jeremiah 29:11)

September 14

I declare that I am resting in the peace that only God can provide, and I will not be shaken.

Truly he is my rock and my salvation; he is my fortress, I will not be shaken.

(Psalm 62:6)

September 15

I declare that God's peace reigns over my home and family, and fear has no place here.

The Lord gives strength to his people; the Lord blesses his people with peace.

(Psalm 29:11)

September 16

I declare that I will not fear the unknown, for God's Spirit gives me power, love, and a sound mind.

For the Spirit God gave us does not make us timid, but gives us power, love and self-discipline.

(2 Timothy 1:7)

September 17

I declare that I am at peace with God's timing, trusting that He is never late.

The Lord is not slow in keeping his promise, as some understand slowness. Instead he is patient with you, not wanting anyone to perish.

(2 Peter 3:9)

September 18

I declare that God is my refuge and my strength, a present help in times of trouble.

God is our refuge and strength, an ever-present help in trouble.

(Psalm 46:1)

September 19

I declare that I will lie down in peace, knowing God watches over me and my household.

In peace I will lie down and sleep, for you alone, Lord, make me dwell in safety.

(Psalm 4:8)

September 20

I declare that fear has no hold over me, for I trust in God's protection and promises.

When I am afraid, I put my trust in you."
(Psalm 56:3)

September 21

I declare that the peace of Christ rules in my heart, and I will not be troubled.

Let the peace of Christ rule in your hearts, since as members of one body you were called to peace.

(Colossians 3:15)

September 22

I declare that God is calming every storm in my life, and His peace stills my soul.

He got up, rebuked the wind and said to the waves, 'Quiet! Be still!' Then the wind died down and it was completely calm.

(Mark 4:39)

September 23

I declare that I am free from worry because I have cast all my cares upon the Lord.

Cast all your anxiety on him because he cares for you.

(1 Peter 5:7)

September 24

I declare that God has not given me a spirit of fear, but of love, power, and self-control.

For God has not given us a spirit of fear, but of power and of love and of a sound mind.

(2 Timothy 1:7)

September 25

I declare that I will walk in peace today, knowing that God goes before me and behind me.

You will go out in joy and be led forth in peace; the mountains and hills will burst into song before you.

(Isaiah 55:12)

September 26

I declare that God's peace will be my guide, and I will not be moved by fear or anxiety.

Let the peace of Christ rule in your hearts.
(Colossians 3:15)

September 27

I declare that I am anchored in God's peace, and I will not let circumstances dictate my emotions.

The Lord gives strength to his people; the Lord blesses his people with peace.
(Psalm 29:11)

September 28

I declare that God's peace calms my mind and soothes my heart, and I will not be shaken.

Peace I leave with you; my peace I give you. I do not give to you as the world gives. Do not let your hearts be troubled and do not be afraid.

(John 14:27)

September 29

I declare that I am free from the fear of man, for I walk in the confidence of God's love.

The Lord is my light and my salvation—whom shall I fear? The Lord is the stronghold of my life—of whom shall I be afraid?

(Psalm 27:1)

September 30

I declare that fear will not control me, for I am filled with faith and peace from God.

Do not be afraid, little flock, for your Father has been pleased to give you the kingdom.

(Luke 12:32)

October 1

I declare that the peace of God transcends my understanding and guards my heart today.

And the peace of God, which transcends all understanding, will guard your hearts and your minds in Christ Jesus.

(Philippians 4:7)

October 2

I declare that I will live in freedom and peace, for Christ has set me free.

It is for freedom that Christ has set us free. Stand firm, then, and do not let yourselves be burdened again by a yoke of slavery.

(Galatians 5:1)

October 3

I declare that God's presence brings me peace, and I will not fear what the future holds.

The Lord is my shepherd; I lack nothing. He makes me lie down in green pastures, he leads me beside quiet waters.

(Psalm 23:1-2)

October 4

I declare that I am a warrior for God's kingdom, equipped with His armor to stand firm.

Put on the full armor of God, so that you can take your stand against the devil's schemes.

(Ephesians 6:11)

October 5

I declare that I am more than a conqueror through Christ, and no challenge will defeat me.

In all these things we are more than conquerors through him who loved us.
(Romans 8:37)

October 6

I declare that I will fight the good fight of faith and lay hold of eternal life.

Fight the good fight of the faith. Take hold of the eternal life to which you were called.

(1 Timothy 6:12)

October 7

I declare that God strengthens my hands for battle and equips me to overcome.

He trains my hands for battle; my arms can bend a bow of bronze

(Psalm 18:34)

October 8

I declare that I am a soldier in God's army, and I will not be entangled by the things of this world.

No one serving as a soldier gets entangled in civilian affairs, but rather tries to please his commanding officer.

(2 Timothy 2:4)

October 9

I declare that I will stand strong in the Lord and in His mighty power, ready to face any battle.

Finally, be strong in the Lord and in his mighty power.

(Ephesians 6:10)

October 10

I declare that God's weapons of warfare are mighty to pull down strongholds in my life.

The weapons we fight with are not the weapons of the world. On the contrary, they have divine power to demolish strongholds.

(2 Corinthians 10:4)

October 11

I declare that I am a victorious warrior, for God has already won the battle for me.

For the battle is not yours, but God's."
(2 Chronicles 20:15)

October 12

I declare that I will stand firm in the faith, acting with courage and strength.

Be on your guard; stand firm in the faith; be courageous; be strong.

(1 Corinthians 16:13)

October 13

I declare that I will resist the enemy, and he will flee from me because of Christ's authority.

Submit yourselves, then, to God. Resist the devil, and he will flee from you.

(James 4:7)

October 14

I declare that I have been given power and authority to trample on every work of the enemy.

I have given you authority to trample on snakes and scorpions and to overcome all the power of the enemy.

(Luke 10:19)

October 15

I declare that I will run the race with perseverance, fixing my eyes on Jesus, the author of my faith.

Let us run with perseverance the race marked out for us, fixing our eyes on Jesus.

(Hebrews 12:1-2)

October 16

I declare that I am not afraid of the enemy's attacks, for God fights my battles.

Do not be afraid of them; the Lord your God himself will fight for you.

(Deuteronomy 3:22)

October 17

I declare that I will persevere in trials, for God's strength is made perfect in my weakness.

But he said to me, 'My grace is sufficient for you, for my power is made perfect in weakness.'

(2 Corinthians 12:9)

October 18

I declare that I have the shield of faith to extinguish all the flaming arrows of the enemy.

In addition to all this, take up the shield of faith, with which you can extinguish all the flaming arrows of the evil one.

(Ephesians 6:16)

October 19

I declare that I will endure hardship as a good soldier of Jesus Christ.

———•———

Endure hardship with us like a good soldier of Christ Jesus.

(2 Timothy 2:3)

October 20

I declare that I will walk in victory, for God has already overcome the world.

In this world you will have trouble. But take heart! I have overcome the world.

(John 16:33)

October 21

I declare that I have the mind of Christ, and I will not be defeated by the schemes of the enemy.

We have the mind of Christ.
(1 Corinthians 2:16)

October 22

I declare that I am armed with the sword of the Spirit, which is the word of God, and I will speak His truth.

Take the sword of the Spirit, which is the word of God.

(Ephesians 6:17)

October 23

I declare that God is my strength, and I will face every battle with courage and faith.

The Lord is my strength and my shield; my heart trusts in him, and he helps me.

(Psalm 28:7)

October 24

I declare that I am victorious in Christ, for He has triumphed over every power and authority.

Having disarmed the powers and authorities, he made a public spectacle of them, triumphing over them by the cross.

(Colossians 2:15)

October 25

I declare that I will wear the armor of God and stand firm in the face of every attack.

Therefore put on the full armor of God, so that when the day of evil comes, you may be able to stand your ground.

(Ephesians 6:13)

October 26

I declare that I am more than a conqueror, and nothing can separate me from God's love.

For I am convinced that neither death nor life, neither angels nor demons, neither the present nor the future, nor any powers, neither height nor depth, nor anything else in all creation, will be able to separate us from the love of God.

(Romans 8:38-39)

October 27

I declare that I will fight the battles of the Lord with confidence, knowing He is my defender.

Do not be afraid or discouraged because of this vast army. For the battle is not yours, but God's.

(2 Chronicles 20:15)

October 28

I declare that I will rise up with courage and fight in God's strength, knowing victory is mine.

Be strong and courageous. Do not be afraid; do not be discouraged, for the Lord your God will be with you wherever you go.

(Joshua 1:9)

October 29

I declare that I am a warrior of light, and darkness will not overcome me.

The light shines in the darkness, and the darkness has not overcome it.

(John 1:5)

October 30

I declare that I will walk in boldness and authority, knowing God has called me for His purpose.

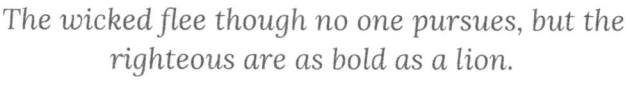

The wicked flee though no one pursues, but the righteous are as bold as a lion.

(Proverbs 28:1)

October 31

I declare that I will be steadfast and immovable, always abounding in the work of the Lord.

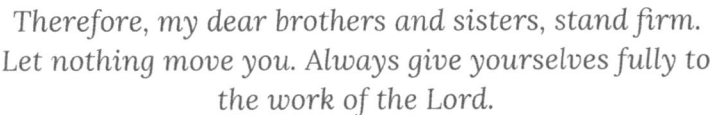

Therefore, my dear brothers and sisters, stand firm. Let nothing move you. Always give yourselves fully to the work of the Lord.

(1 Corinthians 15:58)

November 1

I declare that I am clothed in God's strength, and I will not grow weary in battle.

The Lord is my strength and my defense; he has become my salvation.

(Exodus 15:2)

November 2

I declare that I am a conqueror, defeating every obstacle in the name of Jesus.

Do not be overcome by evil, but overcome evil with good.

(Romans 12:21)

November 3

I declare that I will walk in supernatural wisdom and discernment to overcome the enemy's schemes.

We are not unaware of his schemes.
(2 Corinthians 2:11)

November 4

I declare that I will be a peacemaker, bringing the light of Christ to every situation.

Blessed are the peacemakers, for they will be called children of God.

(Matthew 5:9)

November 5

I declare that God's peace rules in my heart, and I will walk in serenity, even in the storm.

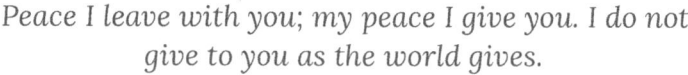

Peace I leave with you; my peace I give you. I do not give to you as the world gives.

(John 14:27)

November 6

I declare that I will persevere in the face of challenges, for God gives me endurance.

Let us run with perseverance the race marked out for us.

(Hebrews 12:1)

November 7

I declare that God is opening the eyes of my heart to see His plans for me.

I pray that the eyes of your heart may be enlightened in order that you may know the hope to which he has called you.

(Ephesians 1:18)

November 8

I declare that I will overcome fear, for God has given me a spirit of power and love.

For the Spirit God gave us does not make us timid, but gives us power, love, and self-discipline.

(2 Timothy 1:7)

November 9

I declare that I will not lose heart, for God is renewing my strength every day.

Therefore we do not lose heart. Though outwardly we are wasting away, yet inwardly we are being renewed day by day.

(2 Corinthians 4:16)

November 10

I declare that I will be victorious over every enemy, for God is my fortress and deliverer.

The Lord is my rock, my fortress and my deliverer; my God is my rock, in whom I take refuge.

(Psalm 18:2)

November 11

I declare that I am fully equipped with the armor of God to resist every attack of the enemy.

Put on the full armor of God, so that you can take your stand against the devil's schemes.

(Ephesians 6:11)

November 12

I declare that I will see miracles, signs, and wonders as I walk in God's power.

Stretch out your hand to heal and perform signs and wonders through the name of your holy servant Jesus.

(Acts 4:30)

November 13

I declare that I will not fear bad news, for my heart is steadfast, trusting in the Lord.

They will have no fear of bad news; their hearts are steadfast, trusting in the Lord.

(Psalm 112:7)

November 14

I declare that I will conquer every trial, for God gives me the victory through Jesus Christ.

But thanks be to God! He gives us the victory through our Lord Jesus Christ.

(1 Corinthians 15:57)

November 15

I declare that I will stand firm in my faith, unshaken by the storms of life.

Though the mountains be shaken and the hills be removed, yet my unfailing love for you will not be shaken.

(Isaiah 54:10)

November 16

I declare that I am a warrior for Christ, and I will stand my ground against every attack.

Therefore, put on the full armor of God, so that when the day of evil comes, you may be able to stand your ground.

(Ephesians 6:13)

November 17

I declare that I will walk in the victory Christ has won for me, for His power is made perfect in weakness.

But he said to me, My grace is sufficient for you, for my power is made perfect in weakness.

(2 Corinthians 12:9)

November 18

I declare that I will be courageous in the face of every challenge, knowing God goes before me.

The Lord himself goes before you and will be with you; he will never leave you nor forsake you.

(Deuteronomy 31:8)

November 19

I declare that I will break through every barrier, for I am an overcomer in Christ.

For everyone born of God overcomes the world. This is the victory that has overcome the world, even our faith.

(1 John 5:4)

November 20

I declare that I will run the race with endurance, fixing my eyes on Jesus, the author of my faith.

Let us run with perseverance the race marked out for us, fixing our eyes on Jesus, the pioneer and perfecter of faith.

(Hebrews 12:1-2)

November 21

I declare that I will not shrink back from the fight, for I am strong in the Lord and in His mighty power.

Finally, be strong in the Lord and in his mighty power.

(Ephesians 6:10)

November 22

I declare that I will see God's faithfulness in every battle, for He is my deliverer.

He delivered me from my strong enemy, from those who hated me, for they were too mighty for me.

(Psalm 18:17)

November 23

I declare that I will stand firm in God's promises, knowing that His word will not fail.

The grass withers and the flowers fall, but the word of our God endures forever.

(Isaiah 40:8)

November 24

I declare that I am victorious because the power of the Holy Spirit lives in me.

You, dear children, are from God and have overcome them, because the one who is in you is greater than the one who is in the world.

(1 John 4:4)

November 25

I declare that I will trust in God's strength and not rely on my own abilities to overcome.

Some trust in chariots and some in horses, but we trust in the name of the Lord our God.

(Psalm 20:7)

November 26

I declare that I am a vessel of God's light, and His light will shine through me wherever I go.

Let your light shine before others, that they may see your good deeds and glorify your Father in heaven.

(Matthew 5:16)

November 27

I declare that I will stand strong in the face of adversity, knowing God is my refuge.

The Lord is a refuge for the oppressed, a stronghold in times of trouble.

(Psalm 9:9)

November 28

I declare that I will overcome every obstacle, for God's strength is made perfect in my weakness.

But he said to me, My grace is sufficient for you, for my power is made perfect in weakness.

(2 Corinthians 12:9)

November 29

I declare that I will not fear the future, for God's plans for me are for good and not for evil.

For I know the plans I have for you, declares the Lord, plans to prosper you and not to harm you, plans to give you hope and a future.

(Jeremiah 29:11)

November 30

I declare that I am a mighty warrior for God, equipped with His power to overcome all challenges.

With your help I can advance against a troop; with my God I can scale a wall.

(Psalm 18:29)

December 1

I declare that God is my rock and my fortress, and I will not be moved by fear or doubt.

Truly he is my rock and my salvation; he is my fortress, I will never be shaken.

(Psalm 62:2)

December 2

I declare that I will run and not grow weary, for God renews my strength each day.

But those who hope in the Lord will renew their strength. They will soar on wings like eagles; they will run and not grow weary, they will walk and not be faint.

(Isaiah 40:31)

December 3

I declare that I am more than a conqueror, and I will walk in the victory Christ has won for me.

In all these things we are more than conquerors through him who loved us.

(Romans 8:37)

December 4

I declare that God is my shield, and He will protect me from every attack of the enemy.

You are my refuge and my shield; I have put my hope in your word.

(Psalm 119:114)

December 5

I declare that God's word is my weapon, and I will use it to defeat every scheme of the enemy.

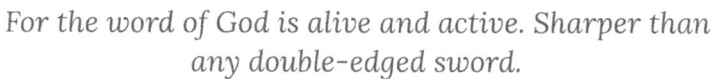

For the word of God is alive and active. Sharper than any double-edged sword.

(Hebrews 4:12)

December 6

I declare that I am walking in God's divine protection, and no weapon formed against me will prosper.

No weapon forged against you will prevail, and you will refute every tongue that accuses you.

(Isaiah 54:17)

December 7

I declare that God is my strength and shield, and He is fighting my battles.

———•———

The Lord will fight for you; you need only to be still.
(Exodus 14:14)

December 8

I declare that I will not shrink back in fear, for God has given me a spirit of power and boldness.

For the Spirit God gave us does not make us timid, but gives us power, love and self-discipline.

(2 Timothy 1:7)

December 9

I declare that I will stand firm in the faith, unshaken by life's storms, for God is my foundation.

Therefore everyone who hears these words of mine and puts them into practice is like a wise man who built his house on the rock.

(Matthew 7:24)

December 10

I declare that God has given me the authority to trample on every work of the enemy.

I have given you authority to trample on snakes and scorpions and to overcome all the power of the enemy; nothing will harm you.

(Luke 10:19)

December 11

I declare that God's strength sustains me, and I will overcome every trial with endurance.

Consider it pure joy, my brothers and sisters, whenever you face trials of many kinds, because you know that the testing of your faith produces perseverance.

(James 1:2-3)

December 12

I declare that I will not be moved by fear, for God is my fortress and deliverer.

The Lord is my light and my salvation—whom shall I fear? The Lord is the stronghold of my life—of whom shall I be afraid?

(Psalm 27:1)

December 13

I declare that I am a warrior for Christ, and I will advance His kingdom with boldness.

The kingdom of heaven has been forcefully advancing, and forceful men lay hold of it.

(Matthew 11:12)

December 14

I declare that God is my victory, and He will lead me into triumph in every situation.

But thanks be to God, who always leads us in triumphal procession in Christ.

(2 Corinthians 2:14)

December 15

I declare that I am more than a conqueror, for nothing can separate me from the love of God.

For I am convinced that neither death nor life, neither angels nor demons, neither the present nor the future, nor any powers...will be able to separate us from the love of God.

(Romans 8:38-39)

December 16

I declare that I will stand firm in my faith, for God has given me the victory through Jesus.

But thanks be to God! He gives us the victory through our Lord Jesus Christ.

(1 Corinthians 15:57)

December 17

I declare that I will fear no evil, for God's presence surrounds me like a shield.

Even though I walk through the darkest valley, I will fear no evil, for you are with me; your rod and your staff, they comfort me.

(Psalm 23:4)

December 18

I declare that I am a soldier in God's army, and I will fight with courage and faith.

No one serving as a soldier gets entangled in civilian affairs, but rather tries to please his commanding officer.

(2 Timothy 2:4)

December 19

I declare that God's peace guards my heart and mind, and I will not be anxious about anything.

And the peace of God, which transcends all understanding, will guard your hearts and your minds in Christ Jesus.

(Philippians 4:7)

December 20

I declare that I will run with perseverance the race God has set before me, and I will not grow weary.

Let us run with perseverance the race marked out for us.

(Hebrews 12:1)

December 21

I declare that God is my refuge, and I will not fear the storms of life, for He is my protector.

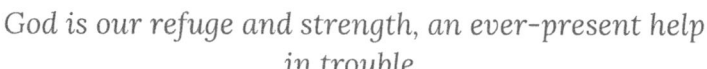

God is our refuge and strength, an ever-present help in trouble.

(Psalm 46:1)

December 22

I declare that I will walk in victory, for God has given me authority over all the power of the enemy.

I have given you authority to trample on snakes and scorpions and to overcome all the power of the enemy; nothing will harm you.

(Luke 10:19)

December 23

I declare that I am armed with God's strength and will defeat every stronghold in my life.

The weapons we fight with are not the weapons of the world. On the contrary, they have divine power to demolish strongholds.

(2 Corinthians 10:4)

December 24

I declare that I am victorious in Christ, for He has triumphed over every power and authority.

Having disarmed the powers and authorities, he made a public spectacle of them, triumphing over them by the cross.

(Colossians 2:15)

December 25

I declare that I will walk in courage and faith, knowing that God has already overcome the world.

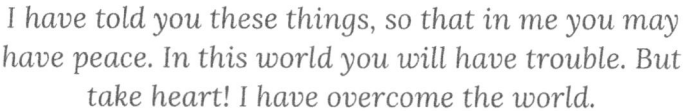

I have told you these things, so that in me you may have peace. In this world you will have trouble. But take heart! I have overcome the world.

(John 16:33)

December 26

I declare that I will stand firm in my faith, for God is my defender and my fortress.

The Lord is my rock, my fortress and my deliverer; my God is my rock, in whom I take refuge.

(Psalm 18:2)

December 27

I declare that I will walk in victory, for Christ has conquered sin, death,
and the grave.

Death has been swallowed up in victory. Where, O death, is your victory? Where, O death, is your sting?

(1 Corinthians 15:54-55)

December 28

I declare that God is my shield and protector, and no plan of the enemy will succeed.

But the Lord is faithful, and he will strengthen you and protect you from the evil one.

(2 Thessalonians 3:3)

December 29

I declare that I am more than a conqueror, for nothing in all creation can separate me from God's love.

For I am convinced that neither death nor life, neither angels nor demons, neither the present nor the future, nor any powers...will be able to separate us from the love of God.

(Romans 8:38-39)

December 30

I declare that I will finish the race strong, for Christ is my strength and my victory.

I have fought the good fight, I have finished the race, I have kept the faith.

(2 Timothy 4:7)

December 31

As we cross the threshold into a new year, I declare that old limitations will fall away and new doors of prophetic, anointed opportunities will swing wide open for me.

Forget the former things; do not dwell on the past. See, I am doing a new thing! Now it springs up; do you not perceive it? I am making a way in the wilderness and streams in the wasteland.
(Isaiah 43:18-19)

ABOUT THE AUTHOR

Roma Waterman is the founder of HeartSong Prophetic Alliance, a thriving online training school that teaches thousands of students worldwide. She is a prophetic voice, worship leader/singer, songwriter and author and is passionate about raising prophetic communities that influence all spheres of society.

As a first-generation Australian, Roma was heavily influenced by her Italian immigrant parents and grandparents. She would often listen to her grandfather play the piano and sing songs of his motherland with love and conviction. In addition to this connection to her heritage, she was also influenced by her time growing up in the church. She not only saw lives transformed, but creative miracles, signs, and wonders were a normal part of her church experience. Her desire to grow closer to God grew daily, along with her love for music.

What she did with those passions has shaped her life and the lives of so many others.

The founder of The Melbourne Gospel choir, she has served as a session vocalist for many television shows as well as a vocal coach for The Voice, The X Factor and Australian Idol. She has recorded many albums and won several international songwriting awards, including The Gospel Music Associations Honour award for outstanding contribution to Christian music, and the 2020 Legacy Award in recognition of outstanding contribution and service to media and the arts.

While these roles have all been incredible for Roma's passion in raising up others, her most prized title has been Mom. However, getting to this place has not been easy. During her early 20s, Roma struggled with endometriosis and fibromyalgia. These painful experiences almost stopped her from being in ministry. Miraculously, she was totally healed. She loves to declare the goodness of God when she speaks of the miraculous conception and birth of her two beautiful kids, Angel and Asa, and loves to pray for others who struggle in this area, where she has seen many healings take place in the lives of others.

Her passion for being a prophetic voice has led her across the globe as a minister, teacher, and trainer, with the prophetic and miraculous being a mark of her ministry. Her passion is to help others receive supernatural blueprints for their lives and she loves to train and raise up others.

Roma holds a Graduate Diploma of Theology and loves teaching on the contemplative practices, Christian meditation and prayer from a prophetic viewpoint. Along with her husband, Ted, they reside in Melbourne, Australia, with their two children and are a part of the leadership in their thriving local church which is currently experiencing a remarkable outpouring of the Lord's manifest presence.

To Find out more about Roma:

Website: www.romawaterman.com
Online Training: www.training.romawaterman.com
Books: https://www.amazon.com/author/romawaterman

www.ingramcontent.com/pod-product-compliance
Lightning Source LLC
Chambersburg PA
CBHW042343300426
44109CB00049B/2734